Extraordina

Written by Hawys Morgan

Collins

Extraordinary pets

Have you ever wanted
an extraordinary pet?
Maybe a dolphin or
an elephant?

Your furniture would not last long with a large elephant in your house!

Let's see which surprising pet could be the perfect match for you.

Salamanders

Salamanders live in lakes and rivers, and on land. They have sensitive skin, so you should not handle them too much.

mudpuppy

Newts

Chinese fire-bellied newts have red speckled stomachs.

They like to nibble on live worms. They can live to be thirty years old.

Frogs

Frogs gobble up bugs and flies like aphids and midges.

All these animals need a large tank with a pool.
If the tank is dry they can catch diseases.

white tree frog

jungle-like leaves

pebbles

puddles

Chameleons

Chameleons have scaly skin and lay eggs.

They change colour in response to changes in temperature, or to hide themselves!

chameleon

Snakes

Royal pythons eat small rodents every 7 to 14 days.

Where is the mouse?

A python will regularly shed its skin as it grows. The entire skin comes off!

Donkeys

Very small donkeys can make lovable pets!

This breed of donkey
is only one metre high.
It is too tiny to ride, but
just right for a cuddle!

13

Hedgehogs

Pygmy hedgehogs come out at night.

They are *very* active.

Arachnids

Arachnids, like spiders,
have eight legs.

Danger!
Toxic sting

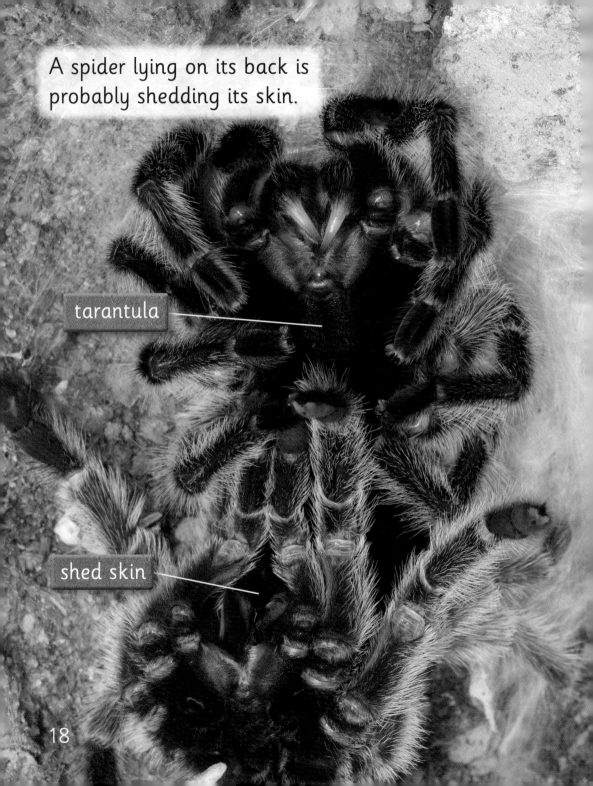

A spider lying on its back is probably shedding its skin.

tarantula

shed skin

Amazingly, spiders can regrow lost legs!

Think about:

Can you feed your pet the right diet?

Do you have a shelter for it?

Is it very active?

Remember! Never choose a wild or endangered animal as a pet.

Whatever pet you choose, be kind and gentle!

Can you match the pets?

newt

donkey

spider

pygmy hedgehog

snake

chameleon

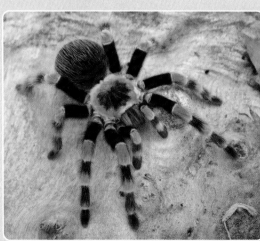

After reading

Letters and Sounds: Phase 5

Word count: 298

Focus phonemes: /ai/ eigh, a /ee/ e-e, ey, e, y /igh/ ie, y /ch/ tch, t /c/ ch /j/ g, dge, ge /l/ le /f/ ph /w/ wh /v/ ve /z/ se /s/ se

Common exception words: of, to, the, are, do, one

Curriculum links: Science: Animals, including humans

National Curriculum learning objectives: Reading/word reading: apply phonic knowledge and skills as the route to decode words, read other words of more than one syllable that contain taught GPCs; Reading/comprehension: drawing on what they already know or on background information and vocabulary provided by the teacher

Developing fluency

- Your child may enjoy hearing you read the book.
- Take turns to read a page of text. Check your child notices the sentences that are questions and exclamations, and uses the correct intonation and tone of excitement or surprise.

Phonic practice

- Point to **Extraordinary** on the cover. Challenge them to separate the syllables as they sound out the word. (*ex-tra-ord-in-ar-y*)
- Take turns to find other long words with more than two syllables to point to and sound out, whilst the listener tries to count the syllables.

Extending vocabulary

- Ask your child to think of an antonym (word or words of opposite meaning) for these. Suggest that they think of just adding or removing letters to create an antonym.

  extraordinary (e.g. *ordinary, normal*)   regularly (e.g. *irregularly, occasionally*)

  surprising (e.g. *unsurprising, expected*)   active (e.g. *inactive, still*)

  sensitive (e.g. *insensitive, numb*)   toxic (e.g. *non-toxic, safe*)

- Can your child think of synonyms for the words above? (e.g. *wacky; shocking; easily hurt; often; busy; poisonous*)

Comprehension

- Turn to pages 22 and 23 and encourage your child to talk through the photos, naming the pets and explaining what they need.